D1625298

Christmas
Cheer

To: _____

From: _____

Christmas Cheer

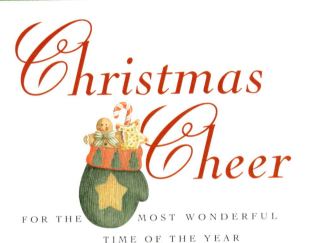

FOR THE MOST WONDERFUL
TIME OF THE YEAR

Vicky Howard

Andrews McMeel
Publishing

Kansas City

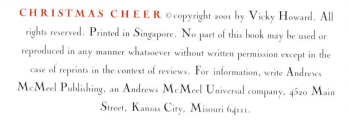

CHRISTMAS CHEER © copyright 2001 by Vicky Howard. All rights reserved. Printed in Singapore. No part of this book may be used or reproduced in any manner whatsoever without written permission except in the case of reprints in the context of reviews. For information, write Andrews McMeel Publishing, an Andrews McMeel Universal company, 4520 Main Street, Kansas City, Misouri 64111.

ISBN: 0-7407-1913-0

Library of Congress Catalog Card Number: 2001086427

www.vickyhoward.com

Book composition by JUDITH STAGNITTO ABBATE
of Abbate Design, Doylestown, Pennsylvania

Christmas Cheer

Christmas is a wondrous time of year. It is a holiday filled with joyous celebrations and traditions that engage all of our senses. Twinkling lights and cherished decorations shimmer in every room. Garlands of popcorn and cranberries brighten fragrant boughs of evergreen. Scents of cinnamon and nutmeg fill the air as gingerbread cookies bake in the oven. Joyful sounds of Christmas carols and jingle bells remind us that the most anticipated time of year is here once more.

From shopping and wrapping to decorating and baking, there is so much to be done! But in the midst of the flurry of activity it is important to pause and experience the magic of Christmas in our hearts. The true spirit of the season is captured in the quiet moments, so take the time to create memories and merriment with family and friends. Deck the halls, trim the tree, bake a batch of cookies, and get cozy in your favorite chair with this collection of illustrated poems, quotes, and recipes. **Merry Christmas!**

*T*here seems a *magic*

in the very name of

Christmas!

— CHARLES DICKENS

*F*eathery flakes are falling,

          f a l l i n g

From the skies in the softest way,

And between are voices calling,

"Soon it will be

Christmas Day!"

— MARY B. DODGE

*M*erry greetings floating
on the frosty air;
Merry faces smiling here,
there and everywhere.

Happiness and holly,
bells ringing clear,
Everyone jolly as
Christmas day draws near.

– The Christmas Entertainer, 1919

12

*B*low the horns, beat the drums,

We'll *all* be happy

when Christmas comes;

Nuts and *gingerbread,* sugar plums.

We'll all be happy when Christmas comes.

— *CHRISTMAS FOR LITTLE LADS AND LASSIES,* 1931

Hang up the holly,

Let Christmas be jolly,

Hang up the greens on the wall;

Have a wreath with a bow,

Some candles to glow,

And a **Merry Christmas for all!**

— MARIE IRISH

A little smile, a word of cheer,

A bit of love from someone near,

A little gift

  from one held dear,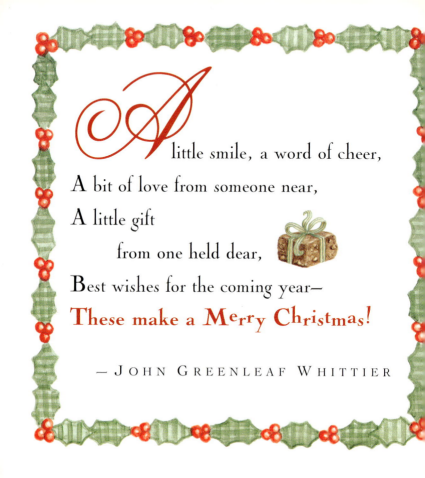

Best wishes for the coming year—

These make a Merry Christmas!

— JOHN GREENLEAF WHITTIER

CANDY CANE RED

*C*hristmas is a pretty time,
     Colors *everywhere* are seen—
Lights and tinsel, stars so golden,
     Brilliant red, and *glossy green.*

SNOW & ICE BLUE

SPRUCE GREEN

STARS OF GOLD

20

The
Colors
of
Christmas

*T*he decorations,

bright and dear,

Bring with them *love and cheer;*

The reds and greens so soft and warm,

We love them *more* each year.

— MAYE CURRIER MINARD

*S*ecrets *everywhere* you go!

Red and green stockings in a row,

Wreaths of holly, bells that chime,

That is *jolly* Christmas time.

— *S A N T A   C L A U S   C H R I S T M A S
B O O K ,   1 9 2 6*

*F*aces bright and smiling

Hearts full of merry cheer—

Oh, that is what makes Christmas

The best time of all the year.

— *CHOICE CHRISTMAS
ENTERTAINMENTS, 1924*

Christmas is a word that contains
everything that makes us *smile*.

Merry, merry

Christmas time,

Have your stockings handy;

Santa Claus will heap them full

With toys and nuts and candy!

— EFFIE CRAWFORD

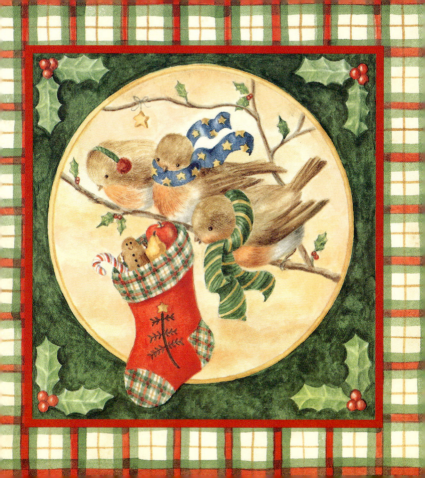

*A*rms are full of bundles

Hearts with love o'erflow—

The real old Christmas spirit

Sets our hearts **aglow.**

— CHRISTMAS POSTCARD, 1915

When we hear others

laugh and sing

we catch the spirit true,

We lift our voices, *join* the throng

And sing of Christmas, too.

— *CHRISTMAS JOY BOOK*, 1925

*C*heerful looks and words are very
sure to make the Christmas merry;
Those that speak the truth sincere,
Hearts that hold each other dear,
These will make a **happy year.**

— ROSSITER W. RAYMOND,
1907

*J*oy is not in things,
it is in us.

— BENJAMIN FRANKLIN

*I*f you would know

true happiness

When comes glad Christmas Day,

Just *give a gift* to someone else

As you go on your way.

— *THE MERRY CHRISTMAS
BOOK,* 1936

Speak loving words
on Christmas day,
Be kind and smiling, too;
Then just keep right on smiling
Each day the long year through.

— SANTA CLAUS CHRISTMAS
BOOK, 1926

#2

CHRISTMAS CHEER

*C*hristmas comes
But once a year,
But when it comes,
It brings *good cheer.*

— OLD RHYME

Up on the housetop the reindeer pause,
Out jumps good old Santa Claus;
Down through the chimney with lots of toys,
All for the little ones, **Christmas Joys.**

*R*eindeer prancing, sleigh bells ringing,
Loads of cheer we know he's bringing;
Happy voices, children singing,
We love old Santa Claus.

— EFFIE CRAWFORD

*I*f Santa Claus should chance to go

   Through country roads adrift with snow,

And see all huddled softly down

   Wild little rabbits, warm and brown,

He'd think what lovely living toys

   To give the nicest girls and boys—

And by their beds he'd like to leave

   The *bunnies cuddled,* Christmas Eve.

— EMILY ROSE BURT

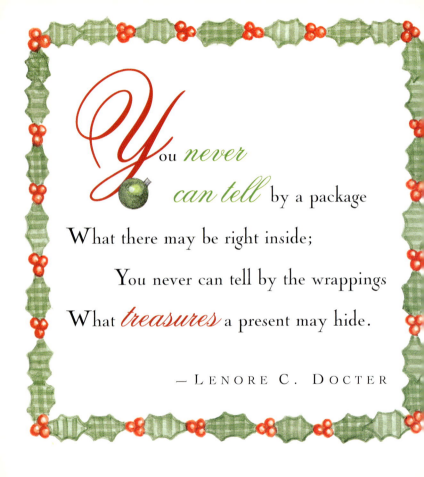

*Y*ou *never*

can tell by a package

*W*hat there may be right inside;

*Y*ou never can tell by the wrappings

*W*hat *treasures* a present may hide.

— LENORE C. DOCTER

Give three cheers for old December,

With his store of Christmas joys,

Bringing *mirth*

and *cheer*

and *gladness*

To a million girls and boys.

— *GOOD THINGS FOR CHRISTMAS*, 1920

*E*verywhere, Everywhere,
Christmas tonight!

— PHILLIPS BROOKS

Christmas is here,
Merry old Christmas,
Gift-bearing Christmas,
Day of grand memories,
King of the year!

— WASHINGTON IRVING

Sleigh bells tinkling—mistletoe—
   Stockings hanging—sparkling snow—
Yule logs crackling—candlelight—
   Spruce trees decked with tinsel bright—
Roasting turkey—mincemeat tarts—
   Merry voices—happy hearts—
Homes where love and joy abide;
   Nothing equals Christmas tide!

— GLADYS LLOYD

MERRY
MERRY

The roofs of homes are blanketed
In dreamy robes of white,
And out through glowing windows shine
The Yulelog's gracious light.
They all sing out that come what may,
To all, a
merry Christmas Day.

— MARIE IRISH

All hearts are home at Christmas.

*H*ome gatherings at Christmas time

Bring those from far away;

How often do long absent ones

Come home for Christmas day.

And if there ever is a time

When people all agree

On one kind, happy, loving thought,

It's round a Christmas tree.

— MAYE CURRIER MINARD

*H*ear the joys bells ring,
       The *happiest* time of year!
O'er the earth they ring,
       Ringing far and near.
Lovely Christmas bells,
       Making hearts so light.
Good will to all the bells ring out,
       A *Christmas song* tonight!

— CHRISTMAS JOY BOOK, 1926

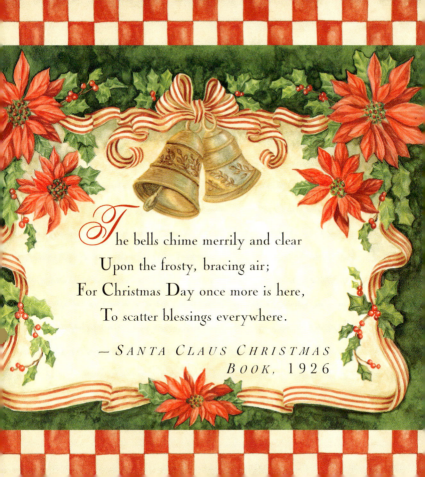

The bells chime merrily and clear
Upon the frosty, bracing air;
For Christmas Day once more is here,
To scatter blessings everywhere.

— *SANTA CLAUS CHRISTMAS BOOK, 1926*

The holly stands for *Christmas cheer*,

And warms our hearts with its bright glow,

For when its shining leaves appear

We're mindful not of chill and snow.

Oh, beautiful Christmas holly!

Hang it high and hang it low:

Emblem of the blessed day

When all hearts with cheer shall glow.

— *GOOD THINGS FOR*
CHRISTMAS, 1920

HOLLYHOCKS

*M*ay you have the gladness of
Christmas which is **hope**;

The spirit of Christmas
which is **peace**;

The heart of Christmas
which is **love**.

— A D A   V.   H E N D R I C K S

Christmas Peace

Bright stars, Christmas stars,

    Shed your silvery light.

Shine again this Yuletide

    As on that Christmas night.

Send the light of heaven

    Into every waiting heart,

Bringing holy Christmas peace

    That *never will depart.*

— CAROLYN R. FREEMAN

*M*ay all sweet
memories of the past,
All blessings
in the present,
All joys that through
the future last,
Make Christmas
bright and pleasant.

— H. M. BURNSIDE, 1910

*S*omehow, not only at Christmas,
But all the long year through,
The joy that you **give** to others
Is the joy that **comes back** to you.

— JOHN GREENLEAF
WHITTIER

Gingerbread Boys

AND

Holiday Joys

The sweetest days of the year are here! And it wouldn't be Christmas without favorite foods and gifts from the kitchen. Enjoy this collection of festive recipes that are sure to make the holidays special.

A Christmas Recipe

I am sending to you a Christmas cake,

I used this recipe.

In making this wondrous Yuletide cake

Which you'll receive from me:

I took a bushel of loving hugs,

And mixed them well with kisses,

I seasoned them with kindest thoughts,

And the *merriest Christmas wishes!*

— CHRISTMAS ENTERTAINMENT
BOOK, 1925

Cranberry Nut Cake

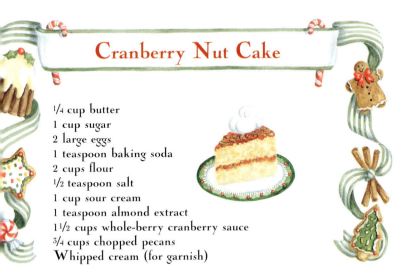

1/4 cup butter
1 cup sugar
2 large eggs
1 teaspoon baking soda
2 cups flour
1/2 teaspoon salt
1 cup sour cream
1 teaspoon almond extract
1 1/2 cups whole-berry cranberry sauce
3/4 cups chopped pecans
Whipped cream (for garnish)

Cream the butter and sugar together, add the eggs, and beat well. Mix the dry ingredients together and add alternately with the sour cream to the egg mixture. Stir in the extract. Spoon half of the batter into a greased tube pan. Swirl half of the cranberry sauce over the batter and sprinkle on half of the pecans. Repeat the layers. Bake at 350° about 1 hour. Let cool and remove from the pan. Garnish with whipped cream.

Santa's Favorite
Sugar Cookies

1 1/2 cups powdered sugar
1 cup butter, softened
1 teaspoon vanilla
1/2 teaspoon almond extract
1 large egg
2 1/2 cups flour
1 teaspoon cream of tartar
1 teaspoon baking soda

Sift the powdered sugar and add it to the softened butter. Cream well. Add the vanilla, almond extract, and egg. Mix well. Sift together the flour, cream of tartar, and baking soda, and add it to the creamed mixture. Refrigerate several hours. On lightly floured surface, roll the dough very thin. Cut into shapes, and place on greased cookie sheets. Bake at 325° about 8 minutes, or until barely golden. Don't forget to save some for Santa!

Candy Cane Confections

Peppermint Brittle

Melt 2 pounds white chocolate over a double boiler or in your microwave. Place 12 candy canes (1 box) in a plastic bag and crush them into small pieces with a rolling pin or other heavy utensil. Stir the candy into the melted chocolate and pour onto a cookie sheet lined with wax or parchment paper. Chill till firm and break into pieces.

Frosted Candy Canes

Melt 1 cup white chocolate pieces over a double boiler or in your microwave. Spoon the chocolate into a pastry bag fitted with a small tip. (A plastic sandwich bag with a tiny hole cut in the corner can be used instead of a pastry bag if you prefer.) Drizzle the chocolate over 12 candy canes and chill until the chocolate is firm. Leave one as a special treat for Santa!

Candy Cane Fluff

¹/₂ cup crushed candy canes (about 6)
1 envelope unflavored gelatin
1¹/₄ cups milk (must be 2% or whole)
3 large egg yolks, slightly beaten
¹/₄ cup sugar
¹/₄ teaspoon salt
red food coloring
¹/₄ teaspoon peppermint extract
8 ounces whipped topping
Whipped cream (for garnish)
1 crushed candy cane (for garnish)

Mix ¹/₂ cup crushed candy canes, the gelatin, milk, egg yolks, sugar, and salt in a saucepan. Cook and stir over low heat until the gelatin dissolves and the candy melts. (Don't bring it to a boil.) Remove from heat and tint with 4 to 5 drops red food coloring. Stir in the extract and cool. Chill until partially set. Fold in the whipped topping. Chill about 5 minutes, until mixture mounds slightly, and spoon into parfait glasses. Chill until firm and garnish with whipped cream and crushed candy cane. Serves 8.

Christmas Candy

For candy that taste as if angels had made it
Of celestial sugar and spice and things.
Tastes as no other kind ever tastes—
I offer you the candy that Santa brings.

— *GIANT CHRISTMAS BOOK*, 1934

Krispy Kringles

9 almond bark cubes (18 ounces)
12 ounces semisweet chocolate chips
4 cups crisp rice cereal
1 cup chopped pecans

Melt the almond bark and chocolate chips in your microwave on high, stirring at 1-minute intervals until smooth. Mix in the cereal and pecans. Drop by the spoonful onto wax paper–lined cookie sheets and chill until firm.

Snowballs

2 tablespoons butter
1 cup packed brown sugar
1 pound chopped dates
2 eggs, beaten
2 cups crisp rice cereal
1 cup chopped pecans
Powdered sugar

Combine the butter, brown sugar, dates, and eggs in a large pan. Heat and stir constantly until the dates begin to dissolve and the mixture is thick. Remove from heat. Add the rice cereal and nuts. With buttered fingers, shape into balls. Roll balls in powdered sugar. Makes 4 dozen.

Christmas Kiss Cookies

1/2 cup butter
1/2 cup chunky peanut butter
1/2 cup sugar, plus extra for rolling cookies in
1/2 cup packed brown sugar
1 large egg
2 tablespoons milk
1 3/4 cups flour
1 teaspoon baking soda
1/2 teaspoon salt
50 Hershey's chocolate Kisses™

Cream the butter, peanut butter, and sugars. Add the egg and milk. Beat well. Add the flour, baking soda, and salt. Beat again and shape rounded teaspoons of dough into balls. Roll in granulated sugar. Place on a greased cookie sheet and bake at 375° for 7 minutes. Remove from the oven and place a chocolate kiss on top of each cookie, pressing so the cookie cracks around the edge of the chocolate. Return to the oven and bake 3 minutes longer. Cool on wire racks and enjoy!
Makes 50 cookies.

Snowfrost Cappuccino

1 1/2 cups milk
3 tablespoons sugar
1/2 teaspoon cinnamon
Dash nutmeg
3 cups freshly brewed coffee
1 1/2 teaspoons vanilla
Whipped cream (for garnish)

Combine the milk, sugar, cinnamon, and nutmeg in a saucepan. Stir well. Cook over medium heat until the sugar dissolves. It takes several minutes, but don't bring it to a boil. Remove from the heat and stir in the coffee and vanilla. Pour into mugs and garnish with a dollop of whipped cream and a sprinkle of cinnamon or nutmeg. Serves 4.

Gingerbread Joys

¾ cup packed brown sugar
½ cup vegetable shortening
1 large egg
1 ½ cups flour
½ teaspoon baking soda
½ teaspoon salt
½ teaspoon cinnamon
¼ teaspoon nutmeg
¼ teaspoon ginger
⅛ teaspoon ground cloves

Cream the brown sugar, shortening, and egg. Sift the dry ingredients together and combine with the creamed mixture. Chill the dough 1 hour. Roll out on a lightly floured surface. Cut out with cookie cutters and place on a lightly greased cookie sheet. Bake at 375° about 7 minutes. Remove to a wire rack to cool. Decorate with icing if desired. Makes about 3 dozen cookies, depending on the size of your cutters.

Friendship Brownies

1 cup sugar
1/2 cup butter
2 large eggs
1 cup flour
4 rounded tablespoons unsweetened baking cocoa
1/4 teaspoon salt
1 teaspoon vanilla
1 cup pecan pieces
Powdered sugar (for garnish)

Cream the sugar and butter. Add the eggs, beating after each. Sift together the flour, cocoa, and salt, and add to creamed mixture. Stir in the vanilla and nuts. Place in a lightly greased 9-inch square pan and bake at 350° about 25 minutes. Dust with powdered sugar when cool. Share a plate with a friend!

"The greatest sweetener of human life
is friendship."

– Joseph Addison

Honey-Pecan Chips

½ cup butter
½ cup honey
1 teaspoon vanilla
1 large egg

1 ¼ cups flour
½ teaspoon salt
½ teaspoon baking soda
½ cup pecan pieces
12 ounces semisweet chocolate
   chips

Cream the butter. Add the honey and vanilla and mix well. Add the egg and beat. Sift together the flour, salt, and baking soda and add to the creamed mixture at low speed just until combined. Stir in the nuts and chips. Drop by rounded teaspoonfuls on a lightly greased cookie sheet. Bake at 375° 7 minutes, or until edges are golden. Cool and store in an airtight container. Makes 36 cookies.

December Cider

¼ cup packed brown sugar
1 quart apple cider or juice
1 teaspoon grated orange peel
¼ cup orange juice
¼ teaspoon whole cloves
2 whole allspice
1 cinnamon stick
1 tablespoon lemon juice
Dash nutmeg

In medium saucepan, over low heat, dissolve the sugar in the cider. Add the remaining ingredients. Bring to a boil, reduce heat, and simmer uncovered 20 minutes. Strain and discard spices. Serve hot. Serves 6 to 8.

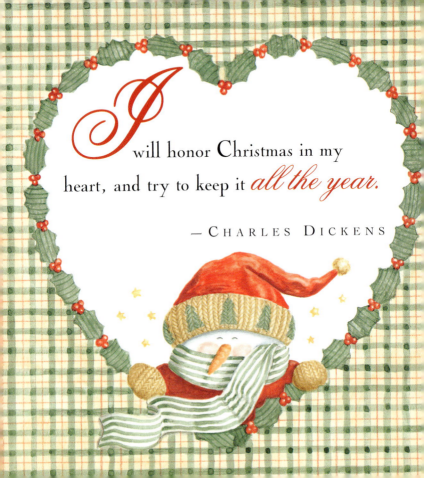

I will honor Christmas in my heart, and try to keep it *all the year.*

— CHARLES DICKENS